W9-AGB-337

Horse Sense

by Beth Gruber

Content Adviser: Professor Peter Bower, Barnard College, Columbia University, New York, New York
Reading Adviser: Frances J. Bonacci, Reading Specialist, Cambridge, Massachusetts

COMPASS POINT BOOKS

MINNEAPOLIS, MINNESOTA

Compass Point Books
3109 West 50th Street, #115
Minneapolis, MN 55410

Visit Compass Point Books on the Internet at *www.compasspointbooks.com*
or e-mail your request to *custserv@compasspointbooks.com*

Photographs ©: Barbara Haynor/Index Stock, cover; Photos.com, 3; Corel, 4; Photospin, 5; Corel, 6 (bottom right); Photos.com, 6 (top right),7; Compass Point, 9 (center left); PhotoDisc, 9 (bottom right); Photos.com, 10,11 (bottom left); Clipart.com, 11 (top left); Corel, 12; Clipart.com, 13 (center left); Corel, 13 (top left); Photos.com, 13 (bottom left); PhotoDisc, 15; Corel, 16,17,18; Martin Rogers/Corbis, 21; Corel, 22 (bottom left); PhotoDisc, 22 (top left); Comstock, 23(bottom left); Corel, 23 (top left), 24 (top center); Photos.com, 24 (left center), 25 (top right); Clipart.com, 25 (bottom right), 26 (top right); Photos.com, 26 (bottom right); Reza; Webistan/Corbis, 26 (left center); Bettmann/ Corbis, 27; Clipart.com, 28 (top center); Corel, 28 (bottom center), 28 (top right), 28 (bottom right inset); PhotoDisc, 28 (bottom right); Photos.com, 28 (left center); Clipart.com, 29 (center right); Corel, 29 (bottom left inset); PhotoDisc, 29 (bottom left); Corel, 31.

Creative Director: Terri Foley
Managing Editor: Catherine Neitge
Editors: Sandra E. Will/Bill SMITH STUDIO and Jennifer VanVoorst
Photo Researchers: Christie Silver and Tanya Guerrero/Bill SMITH STUDIO
Designers: Brock Waldron, Ron Leighton, and Brian Kobberger/Bill SMITH STUDIO and Les Tranby
Educational Consultant: Diane Smolinski

Library of Congress Cataloging-in-Publication Data
Gruber, Beth.
Horse sense / by Beth Gruber.
p. cm. — (Pet's point of view)
Includes bibliographical references (p.   ).
ISBN 0-7565-0702-2 (hardcover)
1. Horses—Juvenile literature. 2. Horses— Miscellaneous —Juvenile literature. I. Title. II. Series.
SF302.G78 2004
636.1—dc22   2004002332

Table of Contents

"From *my* point of view!"

NOTE: In this book, words that are defined in Words to Know are in **bold** the first time they appear in the text.

Equine Evolution

Have you ever dreamed of owning or riding a horse? We may not be soft and cuddly, but we can be loyal, loving, and exciting friends when you learn to understand us.

Horses like me have been around for a long, long time—at least 50 million years before the first humans! In the beginning, we were tiny foxlike creatures. Instead of hooves, we had four toes on each foot, and we stood no taller than 10 inches (25 centimeters) high. Look at us now, and see how we've grown!

Since 3000 B.C., when the first horses were **domesticated** in Central Asia, we have worked beside humans in the field and carried them into battle. Today, however, we also compete in races, shows, and rodeos, and make great companions for owners who simply love pleasure riding.

4

For centuries, horses
have been a source
of artistic inspiration.

5

It's All Relative

Have you ever noticed that horses, zebras, and donkeys share many of the same features? It is because we all come from the same animal family—a family called *Equidae*. Our closest relatives are rhinoceroses and **tapirs.**

All of us have long faces with eyes on the sides of our heads and only one hoof on each foot. We all eat grass and shrubs, and we will travel great distances in search of food and water—or to get away from the flies and mosquitoes that bother us in warm weather. We are animals that were born to run. In fact, we rely on our speed to keep us safe from predators who threaten us in wild environments.

Zebra

Brazilian tapir

Like humans, we are extremely social animals, and we live in family groups called herds. We rarely fight among ourselves, because keeping the peace is important when you live in a herd. However, we will often gently bite and kick other members of our herd to determine who is the boss.

Domesticated horses have many characteristics in common with our wild ancestors. We are herd animals by nature and can easily share affection with other horses or our human family. We **suckle** our young and will always defend our territory. Regardless of our group or **breed,** we are all largely the same under the skin.

Tracing Our Roots

Many of our relatives, like the zebra, come from Africa. However, we horses you know today trace our origins back to the days when Europeans brought their domesticated horses with them to use as transportation to explore the continent.

7

Get to the Points

Horses like me come in many different sizes, but whatever my size, you can measure me in hands. Each hand is equal to approximately 4 inches (10 cm). On average, I stand between 15 and 17 hands high. Any horse under 14 hands is called a pony.

My skull is long and contains 40 sharp teeth designed for grinding grass. You can tell my age just by looking at my teeth. As I age, my front teeth, or incisors, change in shape from oval to round and finally to flat. The older I am, the more signs of wear you'll observe.

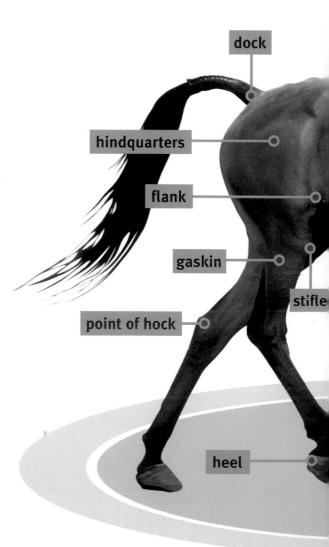

dock

hindquarters

flank

gaskin

stifle

point of hock

heel

mane

crest

poll

withers

forehead

elbow

knee

forearm

cannon

pastern

fetlock

hoof

Like humans, I have a **vertebral** column that protects my back, and a rib cage that protects my heart and lungs. My rib cage, however, runs horizontally, instead of vertically like yours.

No matter what I look like, I share the same body parts or "points" with all horses. Look at the photograph and see how many points you can recognize.

Little and Big

The smallest horse in the world, the Falabella, stands only 7 hands high. The world's largest horse, the Shire, measures 16 hands or higher.

The Way I See It

Although domestication has dulled some of the senses horses used to survive in the wild, I still rely on my acute sight, hearing, smell, taste, and touch to tell me about my world.

Do you need both eyes to see and judge distance? I don't! Each of my eyes has a separate **field of vision** that covers an entire semicircle. I can see in two directions at once, but I do have a blind spot directly behind me. That's why you should never approach a horse from the rear.

Horse Sense

Ever wonder how I can detect something tiny like a fly on my back and then flick it away with my tail? My entire body is so sensitive to touch that I can often feel things a human might miss.

My hearing is super sharp, and my ears move independently to pick up sound waves. When I hear a noise, I lift my head, prick up my ears, and turn my head to see where it is coming from. My body, however, remains pointed forward and poised for flight, so I can run in case of danger.

The membranes in my nose and lips are so sensitive that I can detect almost any smell, from something unfamiliar in my food to the scent of a friend or stranger. Notice how two horses will place their **muzzles** together when they say hello. Smelling is just one more way that I obtain information.

11

All Kinds of Horses

Horses come in many different shapes, sizes, and breeds. Our size and shape, or conformation, along with color and markings, help categorize the different horse families into groups called breeds. We can be black, red or "roan" colored, gold or "dun" colored, spotted, or even covered with different colored patches. Distinctive markings on our faces also help distinguish us by breed. These markings include star shapes in between our eyes and wide stripes called blazes that run from above our eyes to our nostrils.

Every country has its own breed of horse that has been adapted to life in a warm or cold climate and bred for a specific purpose. The more than 200 breeds of horses can be grouped into the following categories.

Group	Characteristics
Hotbloods	Hotbloods, like the Arabian and **thoroughbred**, are slender and fast. An ancient **bloodline** from hot countries in North Africa and Arabia, these high-spirited and courageous animals are the horses of choice for racing.
Coldbloods	Coldbloods, like Cleveland bays, are large, calm, and strong, and are bred for farmwork or pulling heavy loads. The feathery hair around their feet helps keep them warm in the cold northern climates from which they originated.
Warmbloods	Warmbloods, or crossbreeds, can come from almost anywhere. They are bred for temperament and are used for most sporting purposes, except for racing. Most German and Dutch show horses, as well as the American breeds, are warmbloods.

13

Getting to Know You

Unlike most pets that live at home with their owners, most of us live away from home in a barn or a stable. A horse like me might be shared between owners or have regular riders who don't own horses at all! So how do you get to know me, and how do I get to know you?

Take time to introduce yourself. Remember, I cannot see behind me, so always approach from the front and at an angle. Talk to me in a calm voice. Build my trust slowly. If I do not belong to you, ask my owner or an instructor at the stable if I am shy, friendly, or likely to kick or bite. Find out if I am **well-broken.** I am a huge animal, and although I may be friendly, I can also be dangerous. Horses all have distinct personalities—just like people do!

Keeping Company

Companionship is very important to me. I rely on my humans, other horses, and other animals—particularly dogs—to provide the physical contact and mental stimulation I would normally get from a herd. I almost always enjoy a visit from someone who comes to feed, groom, or ride me. In fact, my ability to retain memories will let me know when to expect the people who care for me most.

Home Sweet Home

Even though I may not live at home with you, I still need special care. Whether I am kept on a farm or in a suburb or city, I need a stable to live in and a large, clean stall with comfortable straw bedding. My stall must be cleaned, or mucked out, every day.

Like humans, I need plenty of food and water. I should be fed hay and grain twice a day in winter months, but I can get my own food by grazing on grass in warmer weather. I need to drink 8 to 12 gallons (30 to 46 liters) of water every day—that's 16 to 24 times as much water as humans need!

Wherever I live, I need to be let out into a field at least once a day. Be careful, though. I am amazingly accident prone, and I can be a great escape artist, too. Sturdy fencing made of thick hedges or posts and rails are best for keeping me out of trouble.

I also need to be groomed. Some of us like to be groomed so much, we fall asleep in the process. Others need to be tied with a quick-release knot or **halter** to keep us still. Most stables will have a grooming kit available that you can use to keep me clean from head to hoof.

Horse Health Care

Regular visits from a veterinarian and a **farrier** will help keep me in tip-top shape. Vets provide preventive treatments for common horse ailments like **tetanus, equine flu,** and worms. They also give medicine for illnesses and injuries like **colic** and **lameness.** A farrier should visit every four to six weeks to trim my hooves or replace worn shoes with new ones.

Now 'Ear This

The quality of my relationship with my owner has a lot to do with our ability to understand one another. If you want to know what I'm thinking, look at my ears and face. When both of my ears are pointed forward, I am alert and waiting for you to tell me what to do next, or perhaps a sound has caught my attention. When I am angry, I will point my ears backward and flare my nostrils. Look out! If I am frightened, I will point my ears back, flare my nostrils, and roll my eyes until the white parts show. When I am excited, I will flare my nostrils, arch my neck, prick up my ears, and snort.

Body language isn't the only way that I communicate my feelings. Look at the chart below to find out what I am saying when I "speak."

Horse Talk	What It Means
Whinny or neigh	Is anybody there?
Squeal	I don't want to do that!
Nicker	I am happy to see you.
Loud snort and stare	Is that dangerous?
Quiet, fluttering snort	What's going on?
Scream	I'm furious! Watch out!

I have a special way of communicating with other horses as well. When two horses meet nose to nose and blow on each other, we quickly find out if we will be friends or foes. I will know that another horse wants to be my friend if it nuzzles my coat as it blows back. But if it stomps its front hooves or squeals, I will know to get away.

Horsing Around

How do I know what *you* are thinking? When you speak to me, a soothing, conversational voice can provide answers or reassurance to the questions I ask when I whinny, squeal, or nicker. When you ride me, natural aids, such as your hands, legs, voice, and **seat,** will "tell" me what you want. When applied correctly, these natural aids will tell me when to stop, go, or turn, and when to **walk, trot, canter, gallop,** or jump.

It takes time for horses and humans to learn to understand each other. **Flatwork,** or schooling, helps us both learn how to communicate when riding. Riding isn't the only way that we can have fun together, though. I love to do tricks, and I will get to know you better if you take the time to teach me how to perform some easy **equine** feats.

Ask an instructor how to teach me to bow on command or paw at the ground in answer to a question. Remember to reward me with a carrot or an apple if I do a good job!

If you really want to get to know me, "put yourself in my horseshoes!" One way to do this is by playing a game of "horse" with me. To play, let me loose in a paddock or small fenced-in area. Watch me run around, and then run around with me. We will both have lots of fun and be tired and sweaty when the game is over!

Riding is a good way for horses and people to get to know one another.

Bits and Pieces

As you learn to ride and care for me, you'll quickly learn that I can be a special friend. Here are a few items you'll find essential:

Horseshoes: Good horseshoes are important. After all, I am on my feet all day! Horseshoes are U-shaped metal covers that fit on top of my hooves. They are fitted by a farrier.

Blanket: A sturdy rug or blanket will keep me warm in colder weather. In hot weather, a lightweight nylon sheet will protect me from nagging flies and mosquitoes.

Grooming Kit: I need daily grooming. You will want a good grooming kit that contains a variety of brushes and combs, a sponge, and a hoof pick.

Bridle: The bridle is an open leather cap that straps around my head. It has a bit that fits inside my mouth and is held in place by more leather straps that attach to the **reins**. Riders use reins to help guide me.

Saddle: The saddle is a wooden or metal seat covered with padding and leather that rests on my back. The saddle protects my spine and helps riders balance securely when they are riding. A saddle pad or blanket placed between the saddle and my back will prevent chafing.

Planetary Neighs

I n history, legend, and myth, horses have been regarded as symbols of wealth and prestige around the world.

Horses were considered a measure of prosperity by many Native American tribes and were often both the cause of and the means for waging war. Treasured as both a prized possession and a loyal companion, the horse was often featured with its rider in Native American **pictographs.**

North America

South America

Many graves from China's Han period (206 B.C. to 220 A.D.) contained small horse statuettes. Others used larger horse statues as monuments to mark the graves.

The nomadic Bedouin people would often sleep under the same roof as their horses and share their food with them. The great **sheiks** prided themselves on the beauty of their horses and decorated them with elaborate jewels and cloths.

Europe

Asia

Africa

Australia

The world's oldest horse stables are believed to have belonged to Ramses II, who ruled Egypt from 1304 to 1237 B.C. The large stables, discovered in late 1999, contained a sanctuary and a special bathing area for horses.

Fun Facts Hold Your Horses!

Fasting, Anyone?

There is a breed of horse from Russia called Akhal-Teke that can go for days without food or water.

Snoozing

Horses' legs are built so that they can sleep standing up. To get a good rest, though, they need to lie down.

The Big Sweat

The average horse's stomach can hold about 5 gallons (19 liters) of water at one time. On a hot day, a working horse can lose that much water in less than an hour!

Heavy Hearted

A horse's heart weighs about 10 pounds (4.5 kilograms). A full-grown horse that weighs about 1,000 pounds (454 kg) has approximately 13 gallons (49 liters) of blood in its body.

Speed Diet

Racehorses usually lose between 15 and 25 pounds (7 and 11 kg) in a single race!

Record-Breakers

Can You Believe It?

MINIATURE DWARF HORSE BLACK BEAUTY holds the record for the world's smallest horse. At birth, she was less than 12 inches (30 cm) tall and weighed less than 10 pounds (4.5 kg). In 1996, at the age of 5, the *Guinness Book of World Records* recognized her as the world's smallest horse. She is only 18.5 inches (47 cm) tall.

SECRETARIAT MAY BE THE WORLD'S FASTEST HORSE. His record-breaking 1.5-mile (2.4-kilometer) run in 2.24 minutes at the Belmont Stakes in 1973 has yet to be broken.

THE TALLEST HORSE EVER RECORDED measured 21.25 hands high and weighed 2,976 pounds (1,339 kg). His name was Firpon. Brooklyn Supreme was the world's heaviest horse, topping the scales at a whopping 3,174 pounds (1,428 kg).

TRIGGER, THE GOLDEN PALOMINO that starred with Roy Rogers in dozens of Westerns, was billed as the "smartest horse in the movies." He could perform almost 60 tricks—including counting, doing the hula, untying ropes, knocking on doors, and walking on his hind legs. In 1953, Trigger won the P.A.T.S.Y. (Picture Animal Top Star of the Year)—the animal equivalent of the Oscar.

OLD BILLY IS THE WORLD'S OLDEST HORSE on record. He was born in Lancashire, England, in 1760. He died at the ripe old age of 62 in 1822.

TALK ABOUT STRONG! In 1924, a single shire horse named Vulcan pulled a load weighing 32.5 tons (29.5 metric tons) all by himself!

32.5 TONS

Important Dates Timeline

10000 B.C.   8000 B.C.   1500 A.D.   1600   1700   1800   1900   1930   1940   1960   1990

10000 B.C. Equus, a horse that looks a lot like the modern-day horse, appears.

8000 B.C. Equus disappears from the North American continent. Historians believe these horses were either hunted into extinction or wiped out by a climatic disaster.

1519 A.D. Spanish conquistador Hernando Cortez reintroduces the horse in North America. Native Americans, who have never seen a horse before, are terrified.

1673 Horses and riders provide the first mail service between New York and Boston.

1700s The Conestoga wagon, which is pulled by horses, becomes a symbol of the pioneer spirit.

1875 The first Kentucky Derby is run at Churchill Downs in Louisville, Kentucky. The winner is a horse named Aristedes.

1886 American cowboys ride horses in the first rodeos.

1935 *National Velvet,* Enid Bagnold's classic book about a young girl and an untamed horse, is published.

1938 America's singing cowboy, Roy Rogers, rides into the hearts of American movie-goers on a horse named Trigger.

1961 American TV fans meet Mr. Ed, a horse who can talk.

1990 The first World Equestrian Games are held in Stockholm, Sweden.

Important Horses
Equine Superstars

Some horses are famous for their courage. Others are famous for their speed.

Battlefield Heroes

Marengo was Napoleon's most famous horse. A small gray Arabian stallion, he carried his master in many battles, from the second Italian campaign, through the retreat from Moscow, to the final battle at Waterloo, where he was finally captured. His skeleton is on display in the National Army Museum in Chelsea, London.

The racehorse Man o' War won 20 out of the 21 races he ran. He won one race by an amazing 100 **lengths!**

Racetrack Superstars

Phar Lap is considered by many to be one of the greatest racehorses ever. He won 37 out of 51 races in four years—14 of them in a row! His name is a Thai phrase meaning "wink of the skies" or "lightning."

Seabiscuit, the grandson of Man o' War, won more money than any other horse during the Great Depression. He shattered speed records across the county, winning the hearts of Americans along the way.

A Crow scout named Curley and Comanche, a Morgan-bred **gelding,** were the only United States Cavalry survivors of the Battle of the Little Big Horn on June 25, 1876. Comanche belonged to Miles Keogh, one of General Custer's officers. After Comanche's death, he was stuffed and put on display in the Natural History Museum at the University of Kansas.

Words to Know

bloodline: ancestry

breed: a group of animals within a species that share the same features, such as color or markings

canter: a horse's fast, bounding gait

colic: a kind of stomachache that horses get, sometimes from bad feed

domesticated: tamed or adapted to life with humans

equine: relating to or resembling a horse or member of the horse family

equine flu: a virus that infects horses

farrier: a person who looks after a horse's hooves and shoes

field of vision: the entire area that can be seen without turning the head

flatwork: a system for training a horse

gallop: a horse's fastest pace, during which all four feet can be off the ground at the same time

gelding: a castrated male horse

halter: a piece of equipment that fits over a horse's head for catching, leading, or tying up

lameness: the inability to walk

lengths: units of measure used in horseracing, measuring approximately 10 feet (3 meters)

muzzles: horses' nose and lip areas

nicker: a soft neigh

pictographs: ancient drawings or paintings on a rock wall

reins: leather straps that are attached to the bit and held in a rider's hands

seat: the way a rider sits on a horse

sheiks: Arab leaders

suckle: the sucking method by which an animal gets milk from its mother

tapirs: endangered hoofed mammals that live in South America

tetanus: a dangerous disease produced by bacteria that infect a wound

thoroughbred: a purebred horse

trot: a horse's most natural pace

vertebral: relating to the backbone

walk: a horse's slowest pace

well-broken: trained to obey

whinny: a low, gentle sound made by a horse

Where to Learn More

At the Library

Budd, Jackie. *Horses.* Boston: Kingfisher, 1995.

Clutton-Brock, Juliet. *Horse: An Eyewitness Book.* New York: Dorling Kindersley Limited, 2000.

Ransford, Sandy. *Horses & Ponies.* New York: Larousse Kingfisher Chambers, Inc., 2001.

On the Web

For more information on horses, use FactHound to track down Web sites related to this book.

1. Go to *www.facthound.com*

2. Type in a search word related to this book or this book ID: 0756507022.

3. Click the *Fetch It* button.

Your trusty FactHound will fetch the best Web sites for you!

On the Road

Appaloosa Museum & Heritage Center
2720 W. Pullman Road
Moscow, ID 83843
208/882-5578
museum@appaloosa.com

Hubbard Museum of the American West
841 Highway 70 W.
Ruidoso Downs, NM 88346
505/378-4142
info@hubbardmuseum.org

Kentucky Horse Park and International Museum of the Horse
4089 Iron Works Parkway
Lexington, KY 40511
800/678-8813

INDEX

ABOUT THE AUTHOR

Beth Gruber has worked in children's publishing for almost 20 years as an author, editor, and reviewer of many books for young readers. She also interviews other authors and TV show creators who write for children. Beth is a graduate of the NYU School of Journalism. Her passions are writing and reading. She lives in New York City with her 15-year-old Yorkshire terrier named Kozo.